D0848619

MINI ANIMALS

Babydoll Sheep

by Alix Wood

WINDMILL BOOKS

New York

Published in 2017 by **Windmill Books**, An Imprint of Rosen Publishing
29 East 21st Street, New York, NY 10010

Editor: Eloise Macgregor
Designer: Alix Wood

Photo Credits: Cover, 1 © Alamy; 4, 5, 8, 9 top and bottom, 10, 11, 12, 13, 14, 15, 17, 18, 20, 21, 23, 24, 26, 27, 29 © Bergamascos' Babydoll Brigade ®/Michelle Schubert; 6 © oversnap/iStock; 7 © Jane Cooper Orkney; 9 middle © Circle J Southdowns; 16 © Electrochris/Dreamstime; 19 top © John Carder; 19 middle © Samantha Milner; 19 bottom left © Tomas Hals; 19 bottom right © Chris Turner/Dreamstime; 22 © Alexey Stiop/Shutterstock; 25 © Helen McAteer /Adobe Stock; 28 © Karin Wassink

Cataloging-in-Publication Data
Names: Wood, Alix.
Title: Babydoll sheep / Alix Wood.
Description: New York : Windmill Books, 2017. | Series: Mini animals| Includes index.
Identifiers: ISBN 9781499481495 (pbk.) | ISBN 9781499481501 (library bound) |
   ISBN 9781508192947 (6 pack)
Subjects: LCSH: Sheep--Juvenile literature.
Classification: LCC SF375.2 W66 2017 | DDC 636.3'1--dc23

Manufactured in the United States of America
CPSIA Compliance Information: Batch #: BW17PK. For Further Information contact: Windmill Books, New York, New York at 1-866-478-0556

Contents

Little Babydoll Sheep

This tiny breed of sheep have adorable teddy bear faces. Babydoll sheep are around the size of a Labrador Retriever dog when fully grown. They are easy to handle and very gentle-natured.

Babydoll sheep are usually off-white but can also be black. They are very woolly. Some Babydolls' faces become so woolly they have to be trimmed around their eyes so they don't become "wool-blind!"

Cute Alert!

Some Babydoll sheep have brown or gray **fleece**. They are actually black sheep. Their fleece has lightened in the sun or gone gray with age.

What makes Babydoll sheep most appealing is that they often look as if they are smiling!

Southdown Sheep

A Babydoll sheep's full name is the Babydoll Southdown. The sheep came from the South Downs, an area of Sussex, England. These small sheep **grazed** the downs for hundreds of years. Farmers found their **manure** helped improve the poor, chalky soil. In the 1800s, there were thousands of the sheep on the South Downs.

Sheep still graze on the South Downs. You can see how chalky the soil is by looking at the white chalk cliffs.

Over time, farmers began to use **artificial fertilizers**, instead of sheep, to improve their soil. When World War I began, the shepherds and farmworkers went to war, leaving no one to tend the sheep. During World War II, the downs were used for military training. As a result, the Southdown sheep breed almost disappeared.

After the wars Southdown sheep were unpopular because they were small. Farmers who wanted to breed sheep to sell for meat wanted larger animals.

Robert Mock's Babydolls

Some Southdown sheep were brought to the US. They were popular as they were tough and easy to keep. Gradually, just as in England, US farmers began to look for larger sheep breeds that would provide more meat. Southdowns became less popular.

Farmers in the US began to develop a larger Southdown sheep. They took their largest Southdowns and bred them with other large Southdowns, often from other countries. The breed became known as the American Southdown. The original small Southdowns practically disappeared.

In 1986, US sheep breeder Robert Mock began to search for the original smaller Southdowns. He eventually found a large enough number to start breeding them. He named them Babydoll Southdowns. He bred them to sell to people wanting them to keep as pets.

a tiny Babydoll lamb

American Southdown

Babydoll

Cute Alert!

American Southdown sheep measure between 28-34 inches (71-86 cm). Babydoll sheep measure between 17-26 inches (43-66 cm).

Babydoll Lambs

Female sheep are called ewes. Babydoll ewes carry their young for around 21 weeks. Babydolls will often give birth to twins. They usually don't need any help when the lambs arrive. Sheep are **mammals**, which means their young drink milk produced by their mother. At around one week old the lambs start to nibble a little grass, too. They may stop having milk at around eight or nine weeks old.

Bands put around the lambs' tails make the end of their tails fall off. It doesn't hurt. Having a shorter tail keeps the lamb from getting an illness known as fly-strike.

band

Cute Alert!

A ewe and lamb "baa" at each other as soon as the lamb is born. They learn to recognize each other's voice. This means they can find each other in a field full of sheep.

Babydoll lambs are very cute. They don't have much wool on their bodies, but they have bushy eyebrows, and very thick woolly legs! When lambs run they can look like they are on springs as they bounce into the air. They love to climb and jump onto things.

Friendly Pets

Babydolls are gentle, sweet-natured sheep. Neither the males nor the females have horns. Their size makes them perfect for smaller farms. Babydolls can even live happily in a big yard. They make very good pets.

Babydoll sheep soon start to trust their owners. The sheep like to spend time with people. It won't take long before Babydolls bounce toward their owners the moment they see them. Their faces are very appealing. The sheep's smiling faces usually put a smile on their owners' faces, too.

Cute Alert!

Even the youngest members of the family can help look after a Babydoll sheep.

Sheep are **prey** animals. Prey animals have to be wary of **predator** animals that may want to eat them. To build a nervous Babydoll sheep's trust, you need to spend time with it. Each sheep will have its own personality. Young female sheep are often a little scared of people at first. Male sheep are usually much braver and friendlier.

People often buy **wethers** as pets. Wethers are male sheep that can't father young, so they are cheaper to buy, and very friendly.

Hanging out with your Babydolls when they are young helps build a good, strong bond. Feeding the sheep by hand is a great way to make friends!

Sheep Need Company

Sheep like to live in a **flock**. Their natural **instinct** is to group together with other sheep. A flock will run as a group away from any danger. It is easier for a predator to go after a lone sheep than to pick one sheep out from a large group. Animal experts believe sheep prefer to live in groups of at least five.

Sheep feel safest near other sheep. The best way to calm a sheep in a stressful situation is to make sure they can see another sheep nearby.

Cute Alert! Babydoll sheep get along very well with most other animals, too.

Babydoll owners sometimes put other animals in with their flock to help protect them from predators. Donkeys, female llamas and alpacas, and some breeds of dog make good sheep guardians! Maremma sheepdogs are very popular as sheep protectors. Other types of dog may attack sheep.

Caring for Babydolls

To care properly for a Babydoll, the sheep need to have enough space to live and grass to graze. How much land is needed depends on how good the grazing is. Usually around an acre of good land should be fine for five Babydolls.

Babydolls also need a three-sided shelter to protect them from the weather. The open side needs to face away from the direction the wind usually blows. Their field needs strong fencing to keep out predators.

Babydoll sheep need to have a tree or covered area to get away from the sun. Their shelter may get too warm on summer days. They also need plenty of fresh water.

Bad Hair Days

Babydoll sheep have beautiful, thick wool. Their wool helps keep them warm during harsh winters. When summer comes the sheep need a good haircut to help keep them cool.

Cute Alert!

We can all have bad hair days. Babydoll sheep often get their bedding stuck in their wool!

A Babydoll's wool needs **shearing** at least once a year. It's a good idea to trim the wool around their eyes and tail a little more often. Babydolls need their hooves trimmed at least twice a year, too.

18

Haircuts and Pedicures

Babydoll wool is covered in a special oil that helps keep it waterproof. Too much washing removes the oil. It's important not to wash sheep unless really necessary.

1   Babydolls need some coat and foot care. First, get the sheep used to wearing a halter. This makes them easier to handle.

halter

2   Most people ask a sheepshearer to shear their Babydolls. In between shearings, owners can clip wool away from the eyes and tail using hand shears.

hand shears

3   Hooves need trimming with hoof clippers. A sheepshearer will usually do this for owners, too.

hoof clippers

Useful Wool

When a Babydoll sheep gets a little too woolly, the shearer comes to call. The sheep are usually sheared in spring, just before the hot weather starts.

Sheepshearers usually use electric clippers. The clippers are very sharp. The shearer must take care not to cut the sheep, or themselves! It is a job that takes skill. As one hand clips, the other hand moves around the sheep, pushing the skin taut.

A good shearer will take the fleece off all in one piece. The fleece then is picked and washed. Picking removes any twigs and seeds that are stuck in the wool.

Babydoll wool is one of the finest wools in the world. Many people keep Babydoll sheep purely for the wool they give. People use the soft wool to make clothes such as sweaters, socks, and hats.

Babydolls at Work

Babydoll sheep make great helpers in orchards, berry farms, and vineyards. Other breeds of sheep will often eat a ring around the bottom of a tree or vine, which kills the plant. Babydolls will not do this, but they will keep down the weeds. Pictured below is a flock of Babydolls at work in a vineyard.

Cute Alert!
The main reason vineyards use Babydolls is their height. They can't reach up high enough to eat the grapes!

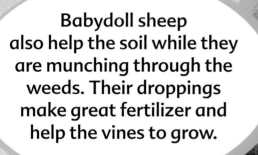

Babydoll sheep also help the soil while they are munching through the weeds. Their droppings make great fertilizer and help the vines to grow.

Babydolls have other jobs, too. Some people take Babydolls to visit people in hospitals and nursing homes. Because the sheep are so friendly and small they make great hospital visitors. Their smiling faces bring cheer to whoever they see.

The sheep need a little training first. They must learn how to be led by a halter and leading rein. They also need to be trained to get used to being transported, and going to a busy, noisy workplace.

Helpful Lawn Mowers

Babydoll sheep make great lawn mowers. Some Babydoll owners even hire out teams of sheep to mow large gardens and cemeteries. The sheep have a lot of advantages over using a normal mower. They will gently nibble around any hidden old stone in a cemetery. A lawn mower would just chew the stone up.

Babydoll sheep lawn mowers are a lot quieter than electric or fuel mowers!

The sheep will work for nothing, and they will happily work all day. Babydoll lawn mowers don't pollute the world with gas fumes, either. Instead, their droppings actually help to improve the grass.

Babydolls have a wider **muzzle** which makes them better lawn mowers than other breeds of sheep. Their droppings are smaller so they spread better, too. Babydolls are less likely to eat shrubs and trees than other breeds. Babydolls are quite happy mowing steep slopes and narrow areas where a lawn mower or larger sheep would struggle to fit.

Cute Alert!

Babydoll sheep lawn mowers won't chew up wildlife, either. This young frog would be much safer with a Babydoll doing the work.

In the Show-Ring

It's fun to enter Babydolls in a show. The sheep are washed and trimmed before their big day. Owners practice getting their sheep used to wearing a halter and leash. The Babydoll needs to get used to noise and being handled, too. It's scary walking into the ring. First-time **handlers** should take some other classes first, to see what will be expected of them in the ring.

Cute Alert!

There are lots of classes sheep can enter. There are classes for ages and breeds of sheep, and for young handlers.

Once in the ring, the handler will arrange the Babydoll's legs so they are not too close and not too far apart. The judge then checks over the sheep. They will look at their teeth and run their hands over the Babydoll to judge it.

The judge will choose a winner. It's very exciting if your sheep wins. Whatever happens though, handlers should always thank their sheep for doing their best!

Test Your Knowledge

1. Babydoll sheep originally came from
   a) New Zealand b) England c) Canada

2. What size dog is the average Babydoll sheep similar to in height?
   a) a pug b) a Great Dane c) a Labrador Retriever

3. Why do owners sometimes clip wool from around a Babydoll sheep's eyes?
   a) the wool is really soft there
   b) so the sheep can see
   c) to make the sheep look good

4. What is a flock?
   a) a type of sheep
   b) a woolly coat
   c) a group of sheep

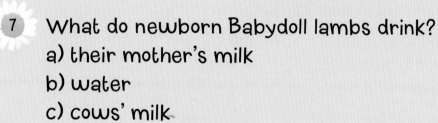

5. Babydolls make great lawn mowers.
a) true b) false

6. When are Babydolls usually sheared?
a) in the winter
b) in the fall
c) in the spring

7. What do newborn Babydoll lambs drink?
a) their mother's milk
b) water
c) cows' milk

8. What are female sheep called?
a) ewes b) thems c) usses

How did you do? The answers are on page 32.

Glossary

artificial Made or done by humans rather than occurring in nature.

fertilizers Substances used to make soil produce larger or more plant life.

fleece The woolly coat of an animal.

flock A group of animals assembled together.

grazed Fed on growing grass or herbs.

handlers People in charge of an animal.

instinct A course of action in response to a stimulus that is automatic rather than learned.

mammals Warm-blooded animals that have a backbone and hair, breathe air, and feed milk to their young.

manure Bodily waste from animals.

muzzle The nose and jaws of an animal.

orphaned Having parents die, especially while the offspring are young.

predators An animal that lives by killing and eating other animals.

prey An animal hunted or killed by another animal for food.

rejected Not accepted.

shearing Cutting the hair or wool from an animal.

wethers Male sheep that have had their reproductive parts removed and cannot father young.

Further Information

Books

Alinas, Marv. *Sheep (In the Barnyard)*.
North Mankato, MN: Child's World, 2016.

Boothroyd, Jennifer. *Meet a Baby Sheep
(Lightning Bolt Books Baby Farm Animals)*.
Minneapolis, MN: Lerner Publications, 2016.

Hasselius, Michelle M. *Sheep (Pebble Plus:
Farm Animals)*. North Mankato, MN:
Raintree, 2016.

Websites

For web resources related to the
subject of this book, go to:
www.windmillbooks.com/weblinks
and select this book's title.

Index

Answers 1) b, 2) c, 3) b, 4) c, 5) a, 6) c, 7) a, 8) a